# The First Battle of Manassas

*A Captivating Guide to the First Battle of Bull Run That Took Place at the Start of the American Civil War*

# Free Bonus from Captivating History
# (Available for a Limited time)

Hi History Lovers!

Now you have a chance to join our exclusive history list so you can get your first history ebook for free as well as discounts and a potential to get more history books for free! Simply visit the link below to join.

Captivatinghistory.com/ebook

Also, make sure to follow us on Facebook, Twitter and Youtube by searching for Captivating History.

# Contents

# Introduction

When the Republican candidate Abraham Lincoln was elected to office as the president of the United States at the end of 1860, his open intention to end the expansion of slavery sent a wave of panic through the Southern states of America, as they relied heavily on slave labor for their plantations. Between December 1860 and May 1861, eleven US states seceded from the federal government to form an unrecognized, independent Confederate government. Not willing to negotiate on the issue of slavery, which had been abolished in the rest of the Western world decades before (for instance, the abolition of slavery in most British colonies had occurred in August of 1834, including the Caribbean), Southern militias began open warfare with their previous government by attacking Fort Sumter in Charleston, which was located within the Confederate state of South Carolina, in April of 1861. This attack was the official start of the American Civil War—only later named as such since both the Northerners and Southerners intended the fighting to be short and decisive, with both sides expecting to be the victors.

After Fort Sumter, the Northerners reached a fervor of desiring a confrontation with the Southern Rebels as the pre-war statement "On to Richmond!" echoed through the North, a sentiment that was driven strongly by the press, the general public, and by certain political elites.

Many seasoned military generals advised against the war or at least suggested a significant delay in order to gather and train troops. These veterans' warnings were ignored, as military field seniors and their troops, as well as President Lincoln and his cabinet, were swept up in the tide of teaching the states that had seceded a lesson they would never forget. The Yankees (a pejorative term Southerners used for Northerners) believed that by capturing the Southern capital of Richmond, located deep in Virginia, in one quick, efficient militaristic move, they would quell the South's voice forever. The Northerners were neither correct nor prepared for the next four years of bloody fighting that defined the American Civil War, which lasted from 1861 to 1865. The Northern Union had underestimated the South's degree of determination, as they wanted to protect their sovereign rights and, more specifically, to own slaves.

The First Battle of Manassas, which took place on July 21$^{st}$, 1861, was the first official land engagement of the American Civil War, even though the war officially started with the bombing of Fort Sumter in Charleston. At the Battle of First Manassas, approximately seventy thousand Union and Confederate troops met near the strategic Manassas Railroad Junction, which linked the vital food-producing farmlands of the Shenandoah Valley to the west with the slave market of Alexandria on the Potomac River to the east and, more importantly, sent rail links south into Virginia and the other Southern states. The Union Army, having approached from the capital of Washington, DC, was required to cross the Bull Run River (or Bull Run Creek) to face the enemy. Thus, the battle became known to the Northerners as the First Battle of Bull Run.

The troops on both sides were "green" and underprepared. The terrain was difficult to navigate, and the approach to the battlefield was long and arduous, especially for the Northerners. The approximate final numbers that came close to the battlefield were 28,450 on the Union side and 32,230 on the Confederate side of the total 35,000 and 34,000 combatants, respectively. Only approximately half of the engaged troops saw direct combat, which resulted in the relatively low causalities for such a heated battle (4,878 wounded, dead, and missing combined).

Confederate General Pierre Gustave Toutant-Beauregard (better known as P. G. T. Beauregard; 1818–1893), who led the Southerners, had tactical control and could engage more of his field since they fought on home ground. Civilians, including close relatives of the soldiers, the press, and politicians, joined in that day and lined the battlefields to take notes, observe, sketch, sell food, or simply enjoy a day out with a picnic and brandy!

The horrifying death and destruction that ensued sent stunned civilians and beleaguered soldiers hurrying back to the capital with the realization that the war to come would be long, bloody, and hard-won. Although the Southerners were the victors of the First Battle of Manassas, they retreated to regroup and strategize. Both the Union and the insurgent Confederacy had learned significant and humbling lessons on that fateful day in July 1861. Both sides withdrew to deal with their injured pride, make difficult decisions that would take the war forward, garner resources for the long fight, and build up more substantial fighting armies than the fledglings they had let loose.

In an ideal world, the carnage at the First Battle of Manassas would have sent the leaders of the North and South to the negotiation table rather than the war office, but sadly, it did not, and both sides became more resolved than ever to destroy their enemies who had, until so recently, been their allies.

# Chapter 1 – A Short Background on Manassas

The Battle of First Manassas (also written as the First Battle of Manassas) is known as the First Battle of Bull Run in the North, and it was fought on July 21ˢᵗ, 1861, in northeastern Virginia within the counties of Fairfax and Prince William. The battle occurred by the Bull Run River, which runs in a southeasterly direction and separates the counties of Prince William on the west and Fairfax on the east. Both armies were over-confident and underprepared, but ultimately, the Confederates won the day by overrunning the Union Army with fresh reinforcements. The First Battle of Bull Run was a staggering and embarrassing defeat for the Northerners, but an anonymous correspondent for the *Atlantic Monthly* (a Boston-based literary and cultural magazine) cast light on this early defeat by stating, "Bull Run was in no sense a disaster...we not only deserved it, but needed it...Far from being disheartened by it, it should give us new confidence in our cause."

His words would prove prophetic, as the Federal Army (the Northern, US, or Union Army) began preparing for a real war in which they would ultimately be the victors. The North's previous attitudes to the newly formed Confederacy had largely been that the rebellious South would quickly and easily be quelled. Those who knew differently and who had been engaged in the War of 1812, which was part of the Napoleonic Wars, were unfortunately too old, for the most part, to be included tactically within the American Civil War.

The sixteenth American president, Abraham Lincoln (in off. March 1861–April 1865), had been snuck into office under cover of darkness to protect his identity and prevent any potential assassination attempts. This was in stark contrast to the future Confederate President Jefferson Davis (1808–1889), who served for the duration of the Civil War and was greeted in Richmond, Virginia, a few months later in 1861 with a brass band and crowds of civilians throwing flowers his way. Davis had been a United States senator from Mississippi for four years before the war, and he also served as the US secretary of war from 1853 to 1857.

Lincoln's election to office is considered as one of the causes of the American Civil War, although the origins of the war were many and were not only deeply entrenched within American society but had also been long in the making. The true causes of the Civil War are still debated and cannot, in truth, be attributed to a single person or event. At the time of Lincoln's election, there were thirty-four American states, with the Northern and Pacific states being largely supportive of his policies, particularly in regards to the abolition of slavery. The Southern states required slave labor (specifically the descendants of African slaves) for their large plantations and to support their heavy reliance on an agricultural economy, mostly in cotton.

President Lincoln was intent upon preventing the spread of slavery into newly acquired American lands and territories that extended toward the west and southwest of the country. The Southerners, in opposition to Lincoln's views, began seceding from the Union to form the Confederate States of America. This secession was not recognized by the federal government nor by the international community and led to the American Civil War, as Lincoln sought to reincorporate the South into the Union and find a solution to the issue of slavery.

The Confederate States of America (CSA) lasted for the duration of the Civil War. The eleven states that eventually broke away from the Union—South Carolina, Mississippi, Florida, Alabama, Georgia, Louisiana, Texas, Virginia, Arkansas, Tennessee, and North Carolina—were all within the "Deep South" of the United States, particularly toward the southeastern extremities of North America. The Confederacy was originally created with only seven states, with Virginia, Arkansas, Tennessee, and North Carolina joining after the official start of the Civil War in April 1861 (and the attack on Fort Sumter in South Carolina). The Confederate capital was moved on May 29th, 1861, from Montgomery, Alabama, to the far more strategic location of Richmond, Virginia, six days after Virginia seceded. Although Missouri and Kentucky technically remained part of the Union, the Confederacy claimed them as their own due to the high number of Confederate sympathizers in those areas, and it ran an illegitimate shadow government in these states.

The nation's capital, Washington, DC (the District of Columbia), on the east of the Potomac River, which essentially formed a dividing line between the North and the South, remained the Union capital during the Civil War. It also became the home of many slaves who fled the South. Washington, DC, was extremely close to Rebel territory, so it was well defended and well fortified during the war.

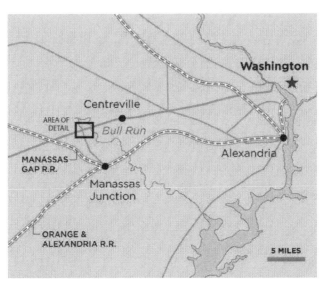

*[1] Geographical context for the First Battle of Manassas in Virginia. The map shows the railroads leading through the pivotal Manassas Junction, the Bull Run River, and the area in detail in which the battle took place. The Union capital of Washington, DC, is shown to the northeast across the Potomac River, surrounded by the state of Maryland.*

The city of Manassas in northeastern Virginia was nothing more than a railroad crossing during the American Civil War, although it was the most strategic rail node for the Confederate Army (also known as the Rebel Army). Manassas Junction, as it was known, linked Washington, DC, eastern Virginia, and the Potomac River with the Shenandoah Valley west of Manassas across the Blue Ridge Mountains. Most importantly, the railroad connected to the Confederate capital of Richmond, which lay 153 kilometers (95 miles) south of the Manassas Junction. The settlement of Manassas grew around the rail junction after the Civil War and was incorporated in 1873—eight years after the end of the Civil War. The Shenandoah Valley was considered the breadbasket for the Confederacy during the Civil War, and while the Confederates occupied it until the autumn of 1864, the valley was used as a strategic juncture from which to launch raids on the Union states of Maryland and Pennsylvania (north of Maryland), as well as haranguing Washington, DC. Despite the fact that the Confederacy was victorious in both the First and Second Battles of Manassas (with the second battle occurring in August 1862), the Manassas Junction and surrounding railroads were controlled by the Union forces for most of the Civil War.

# Chapter 2 – Prelude to the First Battle of Bull Run

The American Civil War officially began on April 12$^{th}$, 1861, when the Confederates attacked the Union stronghold of Fort Sumter near Charleston in South Carolina. South Carolina, which is below Virginia and separated by North Carolina, was entrenched within the "Deep South" but was still vulnerable to attack. Fort Sumter was in reality attacked by the South Carolina militia, not the Confederate Army, as the Confederate Army had not yet been conscripted.

The attack was instigated by the Southerners' insistence that their Ordinance of Secession, which had been ratified by the individual states between the end of 1860 and the beginning of 1861, be recognized and upheld by the Union government. According to the Union government, these resolutions were illegal and unenforceable, as the rebellious states were still technically a part of the United States. As mentioned above, President Abraham Lincoln's election in November 1860 prompted the Southern states to draft resolutions to secede. Lincoln's open opposition to slavery posed a direct and serious threat to the Southern way of life, including their economy and social fabric.

Since Fort Sumter was the start of the Civil War, it is important to look into the battle in a bit more detail. Charleston Harbor, where Fort Sumter was and still is located, is an inlet at the junction of two rivers leading to the Atlantic Ocean and sheltered at the entrance by Morris Island and Sullivan's Island. After the signing of the Ordinance of Secession, the South stipulated that the US Army abandon their position near Charleston, which they did not. The Federal Army was moved, however, by Major Robert Anderson (1805-1871) from the vulnerable position it held at Fort Moultrie on Sullivan's Island to Fort Sumter, which was located on an island that dominated the entrance to Charleston Harbor. The US president at the time, James Buchanan (1791-1868, in off. March 1857-March 1861), sent reinforcements on an unarmed ship, but it was attacked and forced to withdraw. All Union property, except for the fort, was seized by the South Carolina militia. Between January and April 1861, the army within Fort Sumter was technically under siege.

In March, Brigadier General P. G. T. Beauregard, the first general officer of the Confederate States Army, became the commander of the Charleston forces. (P. G. T. Beauregard, who served the US military from 1838 as a brevet major before joining the Confederacy, was also known as "Little Napoleon" or "Little Frenchman" due to French being his first language. He later played a pivotal role in the First Battle of Bull Run.)

Once Lincoln took office, the president decided to send reinforcements to Major Anderson's men during the siege. This, along with the US Army's refusal to evacuate Fort Sumter, led to the bombardment of the fort. Cannons began firing on the fort in the early hours of April 12th, and it lasted for thirty-four hours. The Federal Army was significantly outgunned, and it eventually surrendered, agreeing to evacuate. (No fatalities were incurred on either side during the Battle of Fort Sumter, but unfortunately, there was an accident during the surrender in which a gun explosion killed two Federal soldiers.) The incidents surrounding Fort Sumter were the official start of the American Civil War, although the initial bloodshed of the war was attributed to the Baltimore riot a week later in Maryland, in which sixteen soldiers and civilians lost their lives and hundreds were wounded.

After the start of the American Civil War, newly elected President Abraham Lincoln, who was inaugurated on March 4th, 1861, called on his loyalists for support and requested seventy-five thousand volunteers to aid his efforts to quell the rebellious South (the US Army at that time stood at about fifteen thousand). Lincoln officially issued a proclamation on April 15th, 1861, a few days after the bombardment of Fort Sumter, declaring the South's actions as an insurrection against the United States.

Virginia was one of the states that seceded, and it was a key state by virtue of its strategic proximity to the US capital of Washington, DC. Since the capital was surrounded by the state of Maryland—a slave-owning region that could potentially have become part of the Confederacy—Lincoln worked hard to prevent losing Maryland to the South. He ultimately achieved this by imprisoning secessionist ringleaders, and he narrowly prevented Washington, DC, from being surrounded by enemy territory during the war. The federal capital remained close to the front lines of the fighting during the Civil War and saw constant influxes of wounded soldiers and escaped or emancipated slaves. DC lay only 175 kilometers (109 miles) northeast of the Confederate capital of Richmond in Virginia.

Federal General George B. McClellan (1826–1885, who served two terms of service for the US military from 1846 to 1857 and again from 1861 to 1864), was given command of the principal Union Army of the Potomac, and he built 53 kilometers (33 miles) of fortifications to protect the nation's capital. The Confederate Army never had any intention of directly attacking the supremely protected capital, but it made a few feints for Washington, DC, mostly to confuse and distract the Northerners. The Confederates mostly fought on the south of the Mason-Dixon Line—the line that separated the northern states of

Pennsylvania and Maryland from Virginia to the south. This demarcation was put in place in the mid-18th century and became the de facto division between the Northern free states and the Southern slave states during the Civil War. (West Virginia, which is south of the Mason-Dixon Line, only separated from Virginia in 1863 to become part of the Union.)

Most of the military leaders of both the North and the South had been prominent members of the Mexican-American War, which lasted from 1846 to 1848. Although the war, like many other conflicts, had multiple reasons for starting, it was kicked off by the US annexation of Texas in 1845, in which America ultimately gained the territory from Mexico. Many of the Southern leaders had gained their experience as members of the United States military, so the Civil War's call to arms was painfully personal on both sides, but it was seemingly inevitable. To reinforce how connected soldiers from both the South and the North were, most senior military men on both sides had trained together at West Point, a military academy in New York, and had served in many wars on the same side.

The First Battle of Manassas arose due to the Confederate Congress's plan to hold its meeting at Richmond on July 20th, 1861. The Northern press and general population wanted their government to take action and tame the insurgent South once and for all before the advent of the congress. War fever had spread across the country, and decisive action was becoming imminent. Thousands of Federal troops were gathering at Washington, DC, although these were mostly unseasoned volunteers who set up rudimentary camps around the capital. Many in the North believed that the capture of the Confederate headquarters of Richmond would end the war once and for all.

There had been little time for preparation or training for both the Northern and Southern troops. The voices of reason that spoke against the war in Congress were largely ignored, such as the veteran military commander Winfield Scott (1786-1866), who had fought in the Mexican-American War and every other significant American war since 1812. As the commanding general of the US Army at the start of the Civil War, Scott's opposing ideas to Lincoln's, as well as his advancing age, meant that he stepped back as the head of the US Army in favor of Brigadier General Irvin McDowell (1818–1885). Scott had misgivings about the appointment of McDowell, as well as about attacking the Confederacy head on. His wise counsel as an experienced veteran was largely ignored since he was too old to join the field. Most importantly, Scott recommended a delay on the advance on Richmond, which ultimately led to the First Battle of Bull Run, since the volunteers who had been called up needed more time to train. Scott had been in favor of relying entirely on the experienced and trained US military core personnel.

On July 4th, 1861, President Lincoln asked Congress for 400,000 troops and $400 million "for making this contest a short, and a decisive one." The North's confidence was so great that soldiers were conscripted for an initial period of only three months. Thirty-five thousand Union troops marched from the capital of Washington, DC, to strike at twenty-two thousand Confederate men on July 16th, 1861, who had converged near the river of Bull Run in northeastern Virginia, doing so to specifically defend the Manassas Railroad Junction that brought supplies and food from the west and north to the Confederacy.

As mentioned, Lincoln employed Brigadier General McDowell to lead the Federal troops south, break the backbone of the rebellion accumulating at Manassas, and clear the way to Richmond. The US president was advised by McDowell to avoid the onslaught since the American troops were not sufficiently trained or prepared for battle. However, Lincoln knew that the same would be true of the Southern forces, so he continued with the engagement regardless. McDowell had been headquartered at the abandoned mansion of the Confederate defector Robert E. Lee in Arlington County at the far northeastern corner of Virginia before he led his troops toward the small settlement of Centreville. (General Robert E. Lee served for the duration of the Civil War under the South's banner, but like many of his contemporaries, he had previously served the US Army, acting as a colonel from 1829 to 1861.)

Centreville, which was forty-two kilometers (twenty-six miles) west of DC, would serve as the intermediary point and temporary headquarters for the Union on their approach to Manassas. Centreville lay eleven kilometers (seven miles) northeast of Manassas, with the Bull Run River lying approximately equidistant between the two points. Their movement was unobstructed by Confederate troops, who had started moving back toward the junction once they'd received intelligence of the Union march.

McDowell reluctantly drove his troops southwest toward Manassas Junction. His Army of Northeastern Virginia formed the corps of what would later become the Union Army of the Potomac. The Union Army of Northeastern Virginia contained five infantry (foot soldier) divisions (the 1$^{st}$ to the 5$^{th}$ Division), which were arranged into three to five brigades each. Most of the brigades had artillery batteries. Artillery batteries could be fixed or mobile (naturally, the approaching army had exclusively mobile artillery), containing heavy gunnery and other long-distance field weapons such as cannons (heavy field guns), howitzers (a variation of the cannon for more indirect bombardment via shelling), rifled artillery (heavy field rifle guns), mortars (portable explosive launchers with short, thick barrels and short-range, high-arc detonation trajectories), and the multi-barreled Gatling gun (similar to modern-day machine guns, firing up to six hundred rounds a minute). The average battery would have six to twelve ordnance pieces (mounted mobile heavy guns).

The generals in charge of the five divisions were, respectively, Brigadier General Daniel Tyler, who commanded the largest 1$^{st}$ Division, with four brigades led by Brigadier General Robert C. Schenck, Colonel Erasmus D. Keyes, Colonel William T. Sherman, and Colonel Israel B. Richardson; Colonel David Hunter led the 2$^{nd}$

Division, containing two brigades headed by Colonels Andrew Porter and Ambrose Burnside; Colonel Samuel P. Heintzelman led the $3^{rd}$ Division, with three brigades headed by Colonels William B. Franklin, Orlando B. Willcox, and Oliver O. Howard; General Theodore Runyon led the $4^{th}$ Division, and he did not have brigades nor divisions for engagement but commanded seven regiments from New Jersey and one regiment of New York volunteer fighters and militia; and finally, Colonel Dixon S. Miles led the $5^{th}$ Division, with two brigades led by Colonels Louis Blenker and Thomas A. Davies.

This original Army of Northeastern Virginia also had a cavalry of about four hundred men and their horses. Typical weapons of the war included edged, personal combat weapons, such as short swords, bayonets (generally attached to the end of rifles), knives, swords, and sabers. There was a general shortage of sidearms, rifles, and muskets, but these typically included both the single-shot and the newly developed repeating muskets, revolvers, pistols, and carbines. Crude rocket launchers, hand grenades, and landmines were also used.

McDowell's troops moved slowly, which gave the appointed commanding officer of the Confederacy, General P. G. T. Beauregard, time to send for additional troops and supplies from the Shenandoah Valley. Aided by a prodigious spy network that had been operating in the Union capital, the Confederate Army was waiting, and it was as prepared as possible for the arrival of the Northern troops. Confederate Brigadier General Joseph E. Johnston (1807–1891) was stationed in the valley, and by outmaneuvering the Federal forces, he was able to march approximately twelve thousand men toward Manassas. Johnston had served as a brigadier general in the US Army from 1829 to 1861, after which time he joined the Confederacy as a general until the end of the Civil War.

Despite the fact that these additional Confederate troops (adding to a total of approximately thirty-four thousand overall) joined the battle in its later stages, it is estimated that both the Northern and Southern armies could only put approximately eighteen thousand of their men to good use during the Battle of Bull Run owing to the awkwardness of the battle scene (in topographical and tactical terms) and the general confusion that accompanied the battle.

In June of 1861, in anticipation of a Northern onslaught toward Richmond, Confederate forces used slave labor to reinforce the exposed eastern approach to Manassas (the Bull Run River protected the northern approach), building an extensive series of fortifications and placing strategically located cannons at high points. Signal Hill, eleven kilometers (seven miles) directly south of Centreville across the Bull Run River, would prove to be a key strategic node of the battles to come. Local plantations and their beautiful homes were used as headquarters, redoubts, forts, and field hospitals, and they protected the east-west orientated Orange and Alexandria Railroad leading to the port of Alexandria on the Potomac River. (Alexandria was the site of an important slave market.)

# Chapter 3 – Skirmish at Blackburn's Ford

The site of the forthcoming battle was a mere forty kilometers (twenty-five miles) west-southwest of the enemy capital of Washington, DC. Although Bull Run flows mostly in a northwesterly to southeasterly direction, the section around which the First Battle of Bull Run occurred was where the river makes a mostly northerly to southerly transit through the landscape, which means that the attack strategies of the two armies included crossing Bull Run from approximately west to east and vice versa. A turnpike road (a toll road), Warrenton Road, from Centreville crossed the Bull Run River at Stone Bridge and eventually formed a crossroad on the western side of the river with Sudley Road before reaching the town of Gainesville. Almost five kilometers (three miles) north upstream of Stone Bridge on Bull Run River was Sudley Springs (Sudley Ford), an unmanned ford that permitted crossing in shallow waters.

The Confederacy was prepared for the arrival of the Union troops. They had received a dispatch via their spy network, which was run mostly by society women and young girls from Washington, DC, that a battle in mid-July was imminent. The Confederacy was aware that by July 16th, 1861, the Federal Army was on the march, and the slow progress of the Northerners gave the Southerners time to send for reinforcements.

General Beauregard—the dashing Louisianan who had heralded a heroic standing through the bombardment of Fort Sumter—was the man assigned to move twenty-two thousand Southern troops—the Confederate Army of the Potomac—to an encampment near the little-known river of Bull Run in order to defend the Manassas Rail Junction. Beauregard's initial plan had been a bold and overconfident one of sending for reinforcements and extra troops to pincer the Federal Army in a dual west and east attack at the enemy's flanks. He intended to encircle and disarm the Northern Army and then march northeast to capture both Washington, DC, and the state of Maryland. However, upon consideration, the protection of the Manassas Railroad Junction became Beauregard's primary concern, and he decided to keep his troops in their original place, but he still called for reinforcements since he knew that his twenty-two thousand troops faced thirty-five thousand Union men. (McDowell's army was the largest ever assembled in North America.)

Beauregard's Confederate Army of the Potomac consisted of seven infantry brigades, containing most of the fighting men (19,500), one cavalry unit (about 1,500 men), several additional legions and regional battalions, and almost 40 pieces of field artillery organized under five batteries (about 800 men). It was also apparent that slaves were forced to fight alongside the Confederate Army. The leaders of the brigades were, respectively, Brigadier General Milledge L. Bonham, Brigadier General Richard S. Ewell, Brigadier General David R. Jones, Brigadier General James Longstreet, Colonel Philip St. George Cocke, Colonel Jubal Early, Colonel Nathan G. Evans, and Brigadier General Theophilus H. Holmes (leading the reserves).

In the Shenandoah Valley to the northwest, Confederate General Johnston was holding his position to defend the crucial agricultural land necessary to feed the South. He was threatened by eighteen thousand Northern troops to his approximate twelve thousand men, which were under the command of Major General Robert Patterson (1792–1881), who served three periods of service for the US Army, with his career ending in 1861. Patterson's men of the Department of Pennsylvania were stationed to prevent access to the capital and, more crucially, to block any attempts by Johnston to send his troops southeast to join Beauregard at Manassas.

In this second and most critical concession for the North, Patterson failed. Both Johnston and Beauregard had been poised to move to the aid of the other upon the start of the engagements. When Union forces officially began moving on Manassas, Johnston responded and craftily maneuvered his troops south to support Beauregard. Patterson's inability to prevent military reinforcements from reaching Bull Run was considered the principal cause of the Union's defeat of this first major land engagement of the war, and it brought Patterson's military career to an end, as he was pressured to leave the army.

Johnston had been headquartered in Winchester, Virginia, 89 kilometers (55 miles) northwest of Manassas and 121 kilometers (75 miles) west-northwest of Washington, DC. When General Beauregard informed Confederate President Jefferson Davis that he needed aid since skirmishes and gunfire were already present along his front lines, the Winchester troops safely decamped the valley to move swiftly toward Bull Run. This was done without any major issues since Patterson had inexplicably moved his troops along the Shenandoah Valley, which meant they were out of the path of the Confederate troops. (Some reasons for Patterson's early withdrawal include his men having reached their ninety-day conscriptions, not having received sufficient supplies from Pennsylvania, and General Winfield Scott, who was then the commanding general of the US Army, requiring him to join up with McDowell's army.)

Under Johnston's orders, Brigadier General Thomas J. Jackson (1824–1863) led his brigade from Winchester on July 18th, 1861, protected by the three-hundred-strong 1st Virginia Cavalry of Colonel

J. E. B. ("Jeb") Stuart (James Ewell Brown, 1833-1864). Thomas J. Jackson is a notable name in Civil War history books, although he might be more familiar to readers by his nickname of Stonewall Jackson, which was given to him due to his role in the First Battle of Bull Run. He served the US Army from 1846 to 1861 as a brevet major and then the Confederacy until 1863. Jeb Stuart is another notable name of the war, and he served as the captain of the US Army from 1854 to 1861, ending his career as a Confederate major general. Both men died in the Civil War.

Overall, the Confederate Army of the Shenandoah consisted of four brigades of three to five infantry regiments, each totaling approximately twelve thousand men, including the cavalry. Each brigade commanded one artillery battery with a further twenty pieces for the general field. The addition of the Shenandoah Army would bring the Confederate total to about thirty-four thousand men—just one thousand short of the Northerners. The battle would be equally pitched, but ultimately, it was possibly the unknown arrival of waves of the Shenandoah men during the critical dates of July 19th to July 21st, just before and during the First Battle of Bull Run, that caught the Union unawares. (In fact, McDowell had been assured via Patterson that the Shenandoah Army had not left the valley!) The Shenandoah troops gave the Confederates fresh reinforcements and renewed strength that the unseasoned Federal troops could not match. Toward the main pitch of the battle on the afternoon of July 21st, when it became apparent that the Confederates would win, most Federal troops chose to flee the battlefield upon their own consideration to the astonishment of the Union generals. The overwhelmed and exhausted Yankees then scampered back to Washington, traumatized by their first real experience of war.

The four Shenandoah brigades were commanded by Brigadier General Thomas J. Jackson, Colonel Francis. S. Bartow, Brigadier General Barnard E. Bee, and Brigadier General Edmund K. Smith (replaced during the battle by Colonel Arnold Elzey, 1816-1871, who served the US Army from 1837 as a captain before joining the Confederacy), respectively. Colonel A. C. Cummings of the Virginia Volunteers was also present on the battlefield.

While Johnston was bringing his men down from Shenandoah and McDowell was organizing his attack plan for the Union, Beauregard moved his troops behind the natural line of defense of the Bull Run River. Confederate President Davis had already ordered all troops to move north from Richmond (153 kilometers or 95 miles directly south of Manassas) and Fredericksburg (97 kilometers or 60 miles north of Richmond). The Confederate troops were spread along the western edge of the Bull Run River for approximately eight kilometers (five miles), from Stone Bridge on the Warrenton Turnpike to Union Mills (a stagecoach point) in the south. Aware that both sides of the military corps were novices, Beauregard spread his troops along the stretch of river that would most likely be the scene of the ensuing battle. He concentrated his troops at the fords (shallow points) of the Bull Run River, which averaged twelve meters (forty feet) wide in most places.

Bull Run had steep banks and deep sections that would have been difficult for even experienced troops to cross. Beauregard had, however, left the northern stretch of Bull Run, from Stone Bridge to Sudley Springs, unmanned. When the fighting began at 10 a.m. on Sunday morning, July 21st, toward the Sudley Road Turnpike, Beauregard, Johnston, and most of their men had already spent hours waiting before the continual sound of gunfire to the north made them realize their mistake in focusing on the lower reaches of Bull Run.

*[2] Overview of the map of the First Battle of Bull Run, showing Union Mills in the south and Sudley Ford in the north. This map was created in 1861 by the chief engineer of the US War Office, Solomon Bamberger.*

McDowell intended to proceed cautiously and planned to move from east to west and attack Beauregard's right flank, as close to the Manassas intersection as possible. However, after arriving at Centreville on Thursday, July 18th, the same day Johnston and twelve thousand Rebels were sneaking out of Shenandoah, the Union general conducted a reconnoiter of the intended approach and decided against this initial maneuver. In McDowell's absence, Brigadier General Daniel Tyler (1799-1882, who completed two terms of service for the US Army, the second during the Civil War) was ordered to take the lead division and probe the roads toward Bull Run—giving the impression that they would take Manassas head on. Tyler was joined by Colonel Israel B. Richardson (1815-1862, who served two terms with the army but lost his life the following year at the Battle of Antietam). Unfortunately, Tyler exceeded his orders, and in an act of insubordination that would later be attributed to the loss of the battle, he allowed his troops to exchange fire with the Rebels across Bull Run.

Furthermore, the overexuberant brigadier general tested the Rebels' defenses at Blackburn's Ford (marked on the 1861 map as "Blackfords Ford"), just south of Mitchell's Ford (located west of Centreville). Blackburn's Ford was 5.5 kilometers (3.5 miles) downstream of Bull Run, south of the pivotal Stone Bridge—a bridge of stone that marked the main thoroughfare to Centreville along the Warrenton Turnpike. The Confederate troops, led by Brigadier General James Longstreet (1821–1904, who served the US Army as a major from 1842 to 1861 before joining the Confederacy), remained hidden in the woods on the western bank. Tyler, wanting to ascertain the extent of the entrenched enemy across the river, moved his force forward toward the river. He was arrogant enough to discharge artillery power and send out troops to encourage front-line skirmishes since he saw evidence of the enemy about.

After this initial onslaught by the opposition, the Confederates leaped into action, using musket firepower to send Tyler's men retreating in confusion after half an hour of fighting. Later that afternoon, both sides unloaded hundreds of rounds of artillery fire on one another across the river to no effect for an hour. Essentially, each party seemed to be testing the others' readiness, capabilities, and resources.

The Confederate infantry at Blackburn's Ford was later joined by more troops and artillery, thinking that the main battle had begun. Confederate Colonel Jubal A. Early (1816–1894, who served two terms in the US Army before switching allegiance to the Confederacy during the Civil War, ending his career as a major general) had marched his brigade for three kilometers (two miles) from the headquarters at the McLean House (owned by William McLean, a retired general from the Virginia militia). On the other side, Union Major General William Tecumseh Sherman (1820–1891, who served two periods in the US Army, including postbellum, and would go on to be a key figure for the Federals) arrived late, and his men did not experience heavy fighting.

Unfortunately, the gross inexperience and under-preparedness of all parties were apparent when soldiers allied to the Confederacy sent as reinforcements began firing on their own men at this initial skirmish at Blackburn's Ford. The confusion was connected to the uniforms, as the Southerners were required to wear gray and the Northerners dark-blue, although this coding was not entirely enforced at this point in the Civil War (it remained an issue for the entire duration of the war because the material for uniforms was in short supply). Many volunteers had arrived for battle in their home uniform colors, which sometimes meant Northerners were wearing gray and the Southerners blue! This appalling oversight was listed as one of the contributing factors to the overall confusion of the day since, even under the best conditions, it was difficult to tell foe from friend due to the fighting, yelling, and constant gun smoke.

Eventually, the Union troops retreated under the constant fire of the Confederates. About 150 lives were lost that day on both sides.

Tyler was satisfied that the enemy was in full force and was ready to be engaged at a later point. Although he had completely overreached and even breached his orders, he had ascertained the general positions of the Confederate troops around Blackburn's Ford and had specifically located the extent of their left flank.

Due to the engagement at Blackburn's Ford, McDowell decided not to attack the enemy directly in the direction of Manassas Junction but rather to make a sneak attack from the northwest, far above Stone Bridge. McDowell dispatched his chief engineer, Major John Barnard, to scout a suitable crossing, and he returned with two propositions, including the easily navigable Sudley Ford.

Tyler's foolishness could have potentially undermined the entire Battle of Bull Run three days later since both Confederate leaders, Jubal Early and James Longstreet, later agreed that the Yankees' "licking" at Blackburn's Ford provided a considerable boost to the Confederate Army's confidence, particularly of the soldiers who were young and inexperienced in war. (McDowell's lack of confidence in Tyler also became apparent, and it would play out to the Union's detriment three days later.) Although technically neither side had really "won" at Blackburn's Ford, the disorderly manner in which the Federal troops retreated and the fact that they retreated when they should have never engaged in the first place contributed to the illusion that they had lost.

# Chapter 4 – The Battle of First Manassas Begins

McDowell's decision not to execute a frontal assault on the enemy meant sending his troops far upstream of the Bull Run River in order to close in on the Confederate left flank. This new plan was executed three days later on Sunday, July 21st, since the Federal forces needed to regroup and strategize their main attack plan. This three-day delay was later seen as one of the main causes of the Union loss at Bull Run since the Rebels had time to call for more troops and reinforcements from farther north—specifically Johnston's Shenandoah Valley brigades and cavalry. In the interim, many of the Union volunteer soldiers' ninety days of service had been completed, and they were found by civilians wandering back to Washington, DC, on the eve of the first real battle of the Civil War!

The civilians, excited by the contradictory news that the North had won the skirmish at Blackburn's Ford, were setting out in their private carriages with picnics and champagne to enjoy the final showdown of the war, as, according to their neighbors and the press, it was a battle in which the Yankees were sure to win! Congressmen and press officials joined the civilian crowds to observe and record the ensuing events, which they would later either prematurely report as a Union win, grossly exaggerate, or deeply regret participating in as the battle turned into a rout, with Federal troops sent scampering without permission back to Washington, DC, at the conclusion of the fateful battle.

General Johnston and his commanding units had made haste out of Winchester under Johnston's claim that "Beauregard was being attacked by overwhelming forces...Every moment is precious...for this march is a forced march to save the country." This communique was not true, but it was effective in rallying his troops, who hustled across the Shenandoah River, up Blue Mountain Ridge, and through the Ashby Gap of the Blue Mountains. Jackson's brigade was the first to arrive at the Manassas Gap Railroad Station at Piedmont (now Delaplane), and he loaded as many of his troops as possible into railroad freight cars. The overloaded locomotives took eight hours to cross the last fifty-five kilometers (thirty-four miles) to reach the Manassas Rail Junction in the late afternoon of Friday, July 19th. The rest of Johnston's army straggled into the Confederate camps over the next twenty-four hours, with Johnston arriving at midday on Saturday, July 20th. The last remaining Confederate troops to arrive on the day of battle (Sunday, July 21st) were Brigadier General Edmund Kirby Smith's 4th Brigade of the Army of the Shenandoah.

Johnston, being senior in rank to Beauregard, at first wanted to take command of the Confederate forces, but he later realized this was best left to General Beauregard, as he was more familiar with the terrain. Beauregard's original plan was to cross the lower Bull Run near Blackburn's Ford and, moving from west to east, attack the enemy's left flank.

Ironically, Union Brigadier General McDowell's adjusted plan of moving upriver and crossing Bull Run from east to west to attack the enemy's left flank would have sent both armies chasing each other's tails in a pinwheel movement. McDowell's poor intelligence network had led him to commission the first American aviation unit to aid in his decision of initial attack—this was none other than the United

States Balloon Corps! McDowell employed the services of the *Enterprise*, the first civilian-operated hot air balloon, complete with a telegraph system that provided aerial surveillance of Confederate troops by the Union. (The Balloon Corps was officially in operation for use during the Civil War from 1861 to 1863, but it was never considered to be especially successful.) McDowell is rumored to have joined the civilian aeronaut Professor Thaddeus Lowe in an aerial reconnoiter over the anticipated battleground of Bull Run to make preliminary observations of the field.

The facts of Lowe's participation in the First Battle of Bull Run are contradictory and unsubstantiated, except that he was commissioned in June of that year to survey the surrounding area. Apparently, McDowell, and then later Tyler, were impressed by Lowe and sent those sentiments to Washington. Another account speaks of Lowe being accosted by his allies, the Federal troops, while hovering within firing distance above them during the First Battle of Bull Run. He had not thought to take evidence of his military allegiance when he followed the troops to Centreville. The account—possibly a commission to check on the enemy's movements after the battle on July 24th—tells of Lowe being too afraid to descend in friendly territory because he could not prove his allegiance. He ended up being swept behind enemy lines but made a lucky escape back into Union territory, where he reported that the enemy had retreated and were not making an approach on Washington. Whatever the true account of Lowe's adventures, he was successful enough during this period in the war for Lincoln to approve the Balloon Corps and for more military-grade balloons to be manufactured.

Regardless of the true basis for McDowell's decision to attack via Sudley Springs, it was the correct one. The enemy was located from Stone Bridge southward, particularly around Blackburn's Ford, where they anticipated another full onslaught. At 2:30 a.m. on Sunday morning, McDowell sent about fifteen thousand men under the divisions of Hunter and Heintzelman about five kilometers (three miles) along the Warrenton Turnpike (approximately halfway toward Stone Bridge) to then turn northwest on a road that ran parallel to Bull Run leading to Sudley Springs. (Sudley was located about five kilometers or three miles north of Stone Bridge by a direct route along the river.)

The Northern Army heading for Sudley marched in three columns. David Hunter (1802–1886) was serving his second term of service for the US Army as a major general and marched that day on his fifty-ninth birthday. Samuel P. Heintzelman (1805–1880) had served the US Army for his entire adult life, and he had also finally achieved the rank of major general. Both generals were leading volunteer armies who were not used to marching and had never experienced open warfare. Tyler's division of eight thousand men had been dispatched by McDowell directly toward Stone Bridge to create a diversion away from the bulk of the army marching north, and Richardson's retinue was sent to Blackburn's Ford.

Confusion immediately ensued during both advances from the Warrenton Turnpike. Tyler's 1st Division blocked the forward movement of Hunter's and Heintzelman's 2nd and 3rd Divisions. The 1st Division arrived at Stone Bridge at 6 a.m., but once the 2nd and 3rd Divisions had eventually turned right off the turnpike, they found the route to be little more than a cart lane and stumbled forward in the dark along un-scouted roads. By the time the approximately fifteen thousand northward-moving troops had reached Bull Run at Sudley, it was 9:30 a.m. (two to three hours later than planned). The sixteen-kilometer (ten-mile) approach had included several necessary rest and refreshment stops for the unconditioned troops, which eventually worked considerably in their disfavor as they were spied upon when passing near Sudley.

McDowell's overall plan was to draw the enemy up from the lower fords by sending in Hunter's and Heintzelman's men from the north, allowing the remainder of the Northerners to cross the southern fords and surround the Confederates or at least block the Southerners' movement across Bull Run. The two divisions that McDowell had sent to guard Stone Bridge and Blackburn's Ford were required to execute feints and mock charges to distract and confuse the enemy.

In the early hours of Sunday morning, a Union 20-pounder shell came whizzing into the detached kitchen of the McLean homestead, where General Beauregard was then stationed, near Blackburn's Ford. Nobody was hurt, but Beauregard's breakfast had been ruined. (There are contrary reports that this incident actually occurred on July 18th at the skirmish of Blackburn's Ford at dinnertime.) This was the signal that the battle had begun. A 30-pounder Parrott rifle, a cannon weighing three tons, was also discharged by the Union near Stone Bridge at about 6 a.m., plus more artillery fire from Stone Bridge extending south toward McLean's Ford from the Federal side. (These massive field rifles would later be confiscated by the winning Confederate side.)

Beauregard sent orders to all the commanders stationed along the Bull Run fords, but for some reason, the orders either did not reach the recipients, or they were drastically incorrect. Brigadier General Richard S. Ewell (1817–1872, who served the US Army as a captain from 1840 before joining the Confederacy and went on to play a significant part in the Civil War) was ordered to lead an attack at Union Mills but instead received a message to stand his ground and hold fire. Two other Confederate regiments, including the reserve brigade under Brigadier General Theophilus H. Holmes, were expected to move forward in support of Ewell, but only one received correct orders, which resulted in a single unit moving forward alone. Beauregard's impression was that the battle had begun since it seemed as if a full-frontal attack was occurring along the southern reaches of Bull Run from Stone Bridge downstream to Union Mills. Not knowing that he had, in fact, been fooled by the Union's tactics, he stuck by his original plan of crossing the river to attack the enemy's left flank for several more hours, although it was never executed.

In the interim, Confederate Captain Edward P. Alexander, from his hilltop station on Signal Hill, spotted the Union soldiers near Sudley and sent a timely signal flag warning to Colonel Nathan Evans (1824–1868, who served as a US captain from 1848 until joining the Confederacy as a brigadier general for the Civil War), who was positioned at Stone Bridge with a small retinue of men. (Evans had sent a number of his men to intercept a potential direct threat from Tyler at Stone Bridge, although he soon realized that these were Union feints because of the minimal firing.) Alexander had used the flag signaling method of aerial telegraphy (flag semaphore or wigwag) by using a single flag to transmit, "Look out for your left! You are turned!" A courier scout also arrived from Sudley to get Evans's attention. The Union plan had been to cross the river in the dark and to descend upon the enemy in a surprise attack, but the lateness of their arrival at the ford enabled the signalman to see the sun reflecting off metal as the army moved.

The signaler's message reached Evans nearly thirteen kilometers (eight miles) to the northwest. Evans, taking nine hundred of his men, or eleven of his fifteen companies (as well as his aide, who never left his side and carried a small barrel of his favorite whiskey), rushed north at about 9 a.m. to meet the Union, leaving Stone Bridge pitifully manned with four companies of the 4th South Carolina and two guns.

Tyler's demonstrations, which had been acting as a pinning maneuver to hold the enemy, could have become an outright assault, in which he would have likely overrun the men at Stone Bridge. By 10:15 a.m., the first column of the Federal troops, led by the 2nd Rhode Island Regiment (part of Hunter's men under Colonel Ambrose Burnside), had confronted Evans's 1st Louisiana Battalion on a hilltop behind which Evans had positioned his men with two guns. Matthews Hill, where Evans' men lay in wait, was located in the crook of the northern extremities of the battlefield just south of where Sudley Road met Bull Run.

Thus, the first official frontal engagement of the Battle of Bull Run began. Evans was attributed with considerable courage, as he and his men were vastly outnumbered for several hours while they held off the Union troops and awaited the remainder of the Confederacy. Evans was described as "being everywhere" during the thick of the battle. His leadership was credited as a significant contributor to the South's victory that day. The Confederate forces under Evans spread out on Matthews Hill (above the Warrenton Turnpike and a small tributary leading to Bull Creek) in a thin line, and they effectively blocked the enemy's approach for a time.

At first, the battle on Matthews Hill (a low rise in the landscape) was relatively evenly matched, with soldiers and leaders being wounded, sometimes fatally, on both sides. Major Chatham R. Wheat's (1826-1862, who had served three years in the US Army before joining the South) 1ˢᵗ Louisiana Special Battalion, the "Wheat's Louisiana Tigers," charged at one point, causing confusion in a delaying spoiling attack (an attack meant to disrupt the opposition's plans). The "Tigers" were a semi-mercenary unit organized by Wheat and known for their exceptional bravery and fierceness but also their wild ill-discipline. These approximately five hundred men heralded from New Orleans, Germany, and Ireland, and they were considered socially inferior street fighters. Wheat received a Union bullet straight through his lungs during the First Battle of Bull Run that he ultimately survived—the first recorded in US battle history.

Within an hour or so, reinforcements began arriving on both sides of the battlefield to surge the fighting forward. Union Colonel Ambrose E. Burnside (1824-1881, who finished his military career as a major general at the end of the Civil War before going into politics), leading a brigade under Hunter's Federal 2ⁿᵈ Division, arrived from Sudley Springs from the north. Burnside's men included those under Major George Sykes (1822-1880), who commanded the Regular Infantry Battalion consisting of eight regular army companies from various regiments—the only regulars (official soldiers) in the Union field at that time. Next to arrive at the field was Colonel Andrew Porter of Hunter's 2nd Division and Colonel William B. Franklin of Heintzelman's 3rd Division.

Like Burnside before them, the colonels erroneously sent their men in piecemeal to be defeated in quick succession. Approaching each engagement piecemeal and not engaging the full force of the Union at any point would spell the day's defeat for the Federal forces. However, there was general confusion and poor coordination on both sides.

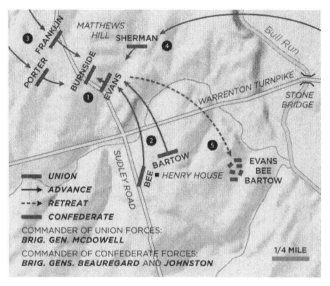

*[3] The start of the First Battle of Manassas showing Evans's troops meeting Union forces near Matthews Hill above the Warrenton Turnpike. The battle would later move south to Henry House.*

Brigadier General Barnard Elliott Bee Jr. (1824-1861, who served the US Army as a lieutenant colonel from 1845 to 1861 before joining the Confederacy) and Colonel Francis S. Bartow (1816-1861, fresh to military service) arrived from the south, having been sent by Johnston in aid of the Confederates. These additions brought the Confederates' total numbers to almost three thousand within the eye of the battle on Matthews Hill, but they were still vastly outnumbered. Neither Bee nor Bartow would survive the day, but both were attributed with courage and their considerable efforts in holding back the Yankees. (They were two of the first most senior officers to lose their lives during the Civil War.)

Bee ignored Evans's orders to stay back, and coupled with Evans's refusal to withdraw, Bee swooped forward to defend the line. Bartow followed to protect Bee. At about 10 a.m., Tyler sent Sherman north from Stone Bridge to join the action on the hill and to attack the Confederate's right flank. The battle of Matthews Hill had turned in favor of the Union, as the Confederates were practically encircled and outflanked, fighting three to one.

Between 11:30 a.m. and noon, the Confederacy began disassembling and moving back beyond the Youngs Creek tributary and the Warrenton Turnpike, and they were covered as they withdrew by Captain John D. Imboden (1823-1895, new to service), who commanded a light artillery unit of 107 men. Southern troops began coalescing around the safety of Henry Hill—a high point near Henry House (home of the Henry family) below the southern intersection of Warrenton and Dumfries (Dumfries, or Sudley, Road led north to Sudley Springs).

When Bartow retreated back over the turnpike south of Stone Bridge toward Henry Hill, he did so with only four hundred remaining soldiers (he had lost at least half of his men). Although the Confederate troops ultimately retreated in sporadic confusion, they had prevented the Union Army from crossing Youngs Creek of Bull Run and then Warrenton Turnpike. The Confederates still retained the critically important objective of the Manassas Railroad Junction. The battle on Matthews Hill had lasted for about two hours, but it was simply the forerunner to the main battle.

Overly enthusiastic observers from the North sent early and incorrect correspondence back to Washington that they had won the day. Without waiting for official military confirmation at the close of the engagement, the Northern press immediately began running stories of success, sending further ignorant observers and civilians toward the battlefield.

# Chapter 5 – In the Heat of the First Battle of Bull Run

The area around Henry Hill was the battle site for both the First and the Second Battles of Manassas, the second being fought almost one year later in late August of 1862. The battle on July 21st, 1861, would rage during the afternoon on the northern grassy open slopes of the 730-meter (800-yard) gradual rise of the hill. (The southern slopes were mostly forested.) The house that topped the hill was home to the eighty-five-year-old widow of Dr. Isaac Henry and her grown children. The bedridden widow, who was unable to leave the house, was mortally wounded on the day of the battle when a Union artillery projectile crashed through her bedroom wall, causing many injuries (and supposedly blowing off her foot). She died later that day from the trauma and was the only civilian casualty of the First Battle of Bull Run.

Union Brigadier General Irvin McDowell had urged his troops south, following the retreating Confederates to regroup just north of the Warrenton Turnpike. Instead of taking the opportunity to hound the enemy south, McDowell took up a position on Dogan's Ridge across the valley, sending volleys of heavy fire to the enemy on Henry

Hill. McDowell hesitated for several hours, continuing to build his reinforcements as his troops still crossed Bull Run.

This delay allowed time for the Southerners to prepare for a battle on Henry Hill, where they formed an army of about 6,500 men (and about 13 cannons), including fresh units from Brigadier General Johnston who had not fought in the morning. At this point, the Confederates were still outnumbered by the approaching Union Army, which was approaching from the north by at least two to one. General Beauregard was also still naturally concerned about the Union forces that remained along the southern sections of Bull Run, as they could cross at any moment to encircle the Southerners from behind. He dispatched Bartow toward Stone Bridge. It would be Bartow's final engagement.

Colonel Bartow rejoined the battle near Henry Hill under the orders of Beauregard to deal with the insurgents over Stone Bridge. His horse was shot from beneath him, and he received a bullet wound, but Bartow simply changed horses and continued the fight. His demise occurred when he rode forward, swinging his cap, yelling to his boys to follow him. He was mortally wounded in the chest and died shortly after on the battlefield. His last words were apparently of encouragement for his troops to continue the fight. The remainder of Bartow's 7th Georgia Regiment obeyed and eventually beat back the fatigued Federal troops, who had been fighting all day. Although the Georgia regiment suffered greatly and had been significantly reduced in numbers, they managed to destroy the enemy battery at Stone Bridge, much to the relief of General Beauregard, who considered it a vulnerable point that made the enemy approach very accessible. (Bartow was posthumously elevated to the rank of brigadier general due to his role in the battle, and his final words of "They have killed me, boys, but never give up" have been immortalized on his gravestone.)

The core nucleus of the Southern army on Henry Hill included "Stonewall" Jackson and his 1ˢᵗ Brigade of the Shenandoah of more than two thousand men. Stonewall positioned his men along the leeward eastern crest of the hill out of the direct line of fire. His thirteen cannons were positioned slightly farther up on the crest of the hill to fire upon the approaching enemy. Behind him was Bee, who would later issue the words that immortalized Jackson's nickname of "Stonewall" in history.

At 1:30 p.m., the overconfident McDowell ordered two Union batteries (under Captains James B. Ricketts and Charles Griffin) up the western side of Henry Hill, which were met at short range by Confederate artillery and musket fire. McDowell had unfortunately sent his batteries of longer-range weapons ahead, whose firepower extended over the heads of the Confederate troops, and the distance was too close for the guns to take effect. The 33ʳᵈ Virginia Regiment leaped from the brush to dispatch with the Union cannoneers and let loose such a volley that an observer described the Union battery divisions' situation as a tragic scene, "It seemed as though every man and horse of that battery just laid right down and died right off."

The surviving Northerners of the batteries drew back to the safety of Sudley Road to rejoin their colleagues but were set upon by a surprise attack by Colonel Jeb Stuart's cavalry on their right flank. The Union guns abandoned on the hill were commandeered by Jackson's men and turned against the Northerners. Under Jackson's command, who told his men to "yell like Furies!" his Confederate troops rushed down the hill, yelling at the enemy as they took ownership of the heavy artillery. It would be the first of the notorious "Rebel yell" that the Southerners used for the remainder of the Civil War.

The Northerners fought back, and at this point, they were still the aggressors and outnumbered their opponents. The Union artillery changed hands again back to their rightful owners. And again, the Southerners swooped down the slope to retake the guns. The Northerners fought back. As the battle rose and fell, each side risked exposing their flanks as they charged. The Union artillery changed ownership several times that afternoon during charge after countercharge, with neither side able to retain their position. The Federals repeatedly fought within meters of Jackson's line, but the general would not budge. He held the line and earned his stalwart nickname.

Farther afield, McDowell's troops had mostly taken command of battlefields surrounding Henry Hill, although, by 4 p.m., his troops were tiring. New troops arriving from Sudley Ford extended the line west across Sudley Road and were showing signs of surrounding the enemy and cutting off their direct line to Manassas.

With the arrival of new Confederate troops in the late afternoon, which joined the focus of the main battle west of Sudley Road, the tide began to turn in favor of the Southerners. The Union Army's insistence on attacking the Confederacy "in bits and pieces" reduced their initial advantage, and by late afternoon, they were no longer in a position to surround the Southerners and forge their way to Manassas Junction.

Union Colonel Sherman had sent two charges up Henry Hill to attack Jackson's right flank (one being the "Highlanders" in their tartan pants), but both had been a failure due to the continual confusion over uniforms and flags. The soldiers' inconsistent attire, as well as the similarity between the Northern and Southern flags that were held aloft of fighting troops, had caused significant hesitation in attacking companies—particularly to the detriment of the Union men, who often found themselves virtually upon their enemy before realizing who they were.

To further add to the confusion over allegiances, the Union Zouaves, the 11th New York Volunteer Infantry (modeled on the French mercenary light infantry companies of the same name), an elite unit organized by Officer Elmer E. Ellsworth (1837–1861, who died before the battle but was a close personal friend of President Lincoln), wore red-striped trousers and fez caps in the likeness of their North African brothers! The Zouaves proved to be fierce, unconventional fighting men who were well-coordinated and trained and remained in the thick of the battle for most of the day. ("Remember Ellsworth!" became a rallying Union battle cry, as the men felt loyalty to Ellsworth's commitment to his men.)

Earlier that day, Sherman was fired upon by Confederate Colonel Wade Hampton III's legion, which had moved in to support the right flank and support Jackson. Hampton's men and horses were fresh but panting from their recent exertion of making their way from the railroad station. His unit contained artillery, infantry, and cavalry (about 650 men).

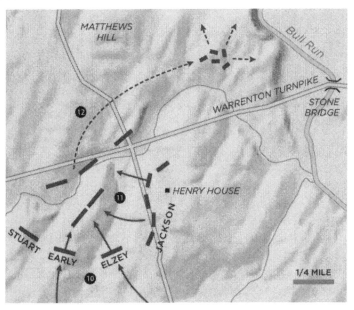

*[4] Final positions of Northern and Southern troops at the First Battle of Manassas in the late afternoon of July 21ˢᵗ, 1861. The Confederates were in a substantially stronger tactical position and were about to win the day.*

The final Union brigade to reach the battle scene at about 3 p.m. was under the command of Colonel Oliver O. Howard of Heintzelman's division. Howard (1830–1909, a career army officer) had been instructed to turn the enemy's left flank away from the main battle. (Until then, he had been stationed to protect Sudley Ford.)

Holding his position on Chinn Ridge, west of Henry Hill over Sudley Road, Colonel Howard was met with overwhelming numbers of Confederate forces that had been sent to swing around the west. The Southern units under Colonel Early and Brigadier General Bonham had been pulled away from the southern fords to join the left flank of the Confederates. The last of the Confederates to join the heat of the battle toward the west was Brigadier General Smith (and, subsequently, Colonel Elzey of the Shenandoah 4th Brigade soon after Smith was wounded), freshly arrived from Shenandoah. The additional Southern units made a crushing full-frontal attack on Howard, who sent his men into battle in small, vulnerable units in waves of unsuccessful counterattacks. (Smith's troops had just completed a ten-kilometer, or six-mile, journey from the train.)

The Confederates had crippled the Union's right flank, and the Federals were in danger of being surrounded, as their exit route north was blocked. Tyler, who had by this point retaken Stone Bridge, for some reason did not bring aid to the Union's left flank, even though he had three infantry brigades and heavy artillery available. (It has been suggested that he never received orders to do so, as McDowell, who was in the heart of the battle, was distracted.)

Similar to the western extremity of the battle, the Federals in the east were also weakening, as Colonel Keyes of Tyler's 1st Division, including 150 men, had been repulsed by the Rebels. On top of that, Confederate Jeb Stuart's cavalry had ridden east to add to the squeeze. When the Confederates saw the Northerners begin to fall back in exhaustion and confusion, the entire Southern line was ordered forward by Beauregard, including the Confederates now in control of Henry Hill. Jackson progressed down Henry Hill, capturing artillery as he moved. Jeb Stuart's artillery swept through sections of the Union, sending them hurrying backward in disarray.

By 5 p.m., McDowell's army was certifiably in chaos and disintegrating. His final orders to Tyler to bring fresh troops across Bull Run to attack the far left, as the Confederacy had done to them in the west, could not be executed because Tyler's pinning forces were already in full retreat—without orders to do so. (Later, some of these units would at least hold the road to Centreville, allowing for the disgraceful Federal withdrawal.)

Panic and disorder had set in on the Northern side, and unfledged soldiers abandoned the scene in an unspecified retreat. It was mid-summer and stiflingly hot in the heat of battle, and the volunteer fighters had lost their romantic notions of the glory of war, no matter how patriotic their original intentions had been. (Essentially, McDowell had led a ragtag crew who were underdisciplined, poorly armed, and poorly outfitted for the job at hand.) As mentioned above, the lack of correct uniforms on both sides had meant troops unleashing firepower on friendlies and sometimes allowing the enemy to approach and overwhelm them, thinking they were allies. The inconsistent uniform debacle occurred many times on both sides throughout the day. To add to the allegiance confusion, the Confederate flag of blue, white, and red with a circle of stars and thick stripes was almost impossible to tell apart from the United States Star-Spangled Banner in the midst of fighting. (The Confederates later changed their flag to a large starred cross, which is still seen in the South today.)

McDowell's and other senior officers' attempts to halt the deserting troops proved futile. He posted rear guards at the various crossroads and fords that marked the retreat of the demoralized troops, who were being harried home in fear. These guards consisted mostly of Porter's men, Sykes's Regulars, and Ellsworth's "Fire" Zouaves of the 11th New York, who experienced heavy casualties as a result. Hordes of Northern soldiers clogged the retreat to Centreville and collided with civilians and their carriages along the way. There were reports of soldiers throwing down their weapons and belongings, stealing horses, and fleeing the scene of battle any way they could. In some instances, the Union retreat became a frenzy, as the petrified soldiers' way out was blocked by exploded and abandoned gun carriages and ambulances. For example, a carriage blocked the bridge over the Cub Run tributary of Bull Run toward Centreville, which created mass panic. Kind citizens in Washington, DC, who received and aided the troops when they eventually arrived in the capital over the next few days, spoke of traumatized, famished, dehydrated men, shaken and half-mad by their first experiences of war.

Dead and dying men and horses, as well human body parts, scattered the battlefields. Dying men had embraced their foes in their last moments. Some of the wounded had simply died of dehydration in the ten-hour-long battle. The local private buildings—churches, houses, and barns—were used as field hospitals and became the sites for horror stories. One Southerner who approached a manor house field hospital described "piles of legs, feet, hands and arms, all thrown together, and at a distance resembled piles of corn at a corn-shucking." The rudimentary facilities and lack of medical help at the time required excessive amputations, often in any space and on any table available, including in grand dining halls or church benches. For those left wounded, slow deaths and gangrene often became their fate, and rampant diseases such as dysentery and scarlet fever swept through sickbays and healthy camps alike.

The Southerners made a preliminary and vague attempt to chase their enemies north and cut off their route to the capital, but they eventually allowed them to flee—but not without sending heavy firepower at their retreating backs. Toward the end of the day, Confederate President Jefferson Davis joined the victorious Beauregard and Johnston on Henry Hill to discuss whether the pursuit of the enemy was advantageous, but in all honesty, the Confederate forces were in similar disarray as their enemy and were just as depleted. So, the Southerners stayed put, regrouping and withdrawing their men over the following days. (A day-long rainstorm on Monday, July 22$^{nd}$, contributed to the Confederacy's decision not to pursue the enemy and also added to the heavy and horrifying atmosphere as Union troops limped into Washington in desperate need of aid.)

Most of the Union artillery abandoned on the battlefields was captured by the Confederates. Beauregard's paranoia about the Confederacy's now exposed right flank toward Union Mills, as well as a rumor that the enemy had turned and was approaching from the southeast, sent the victors hurrying to ensure the Federal forces had not returned. By this time, it was nightfall, and with the hastily retreating and completely shattered Union Army heading home in a rout, which would later be referred to by the Southern press as "the Great Skedaddle," the Confederates had won the day and the first real land battle of the American Civil War.

# Chapter 6 – Retreat and Reprisals

President Abraham Lincoln had remained awake all of Sunday night for news of the battle. Word finally reached him. "General McDowell's Army in full retreat through Centreville. The day is lost. Save Washington and the remnants of this army." Upon hearing this, an emergency cabinet meeting was immediately called, in which Lincoln's secretary of war, Simon Cameron (whose brother had died the previous day at Bull Run) put the nearest town to Washington, DC, Baltimore, which is sixty-four kilometers (forty miles) northeast of DC on high alert in case of an attack, and they also ordered all organized militia to defend the capital. Due to media fallacies, most of the North awoke on Monday morning believing that the North had won, not realizing that the day would be marked as "Black Monday" from thereon.

The federal government was devastated by the news of the loss, more so because it meant a protracted and expensive affair going forward. The Union's original idea to enlist men for a mere ninety days was altered to up to three-year conscriptions, and Lincoln signed a bill for a further 500,000 men to enlist. It was the end of innocence and idealism in the North and signaled the premature end of many career army officers' terms of service—both for the North, where blame needed to be apportioned for the dismal failings at Bull Run, and for the South, for at the end of the Civil War, previous US Army officers were not allowed to serve the Union.

Although Union General Patterson's career was brought to an end due to his failure to prevent Confederate reinforcements from reaching Bull Run from the Shenandoah Valley, General Johnston later admitted that after the enemy's defeat at Bull Run, it was the presence of Patterson's men to the north that prevented him from chasing the limping Federal Army back to Washington, DC, and the incumbent complete annihilation of part of the Union (and perhaps even a frontal assault on the capital).

The First Battle of Bull Run saw the first fatality of a senior officer on either side—Brigadier General Barnard E. Bee. Bee was dispatched under Johnston and was attributed with the nicknaming of "Stonewall Jackson" when he was purported to have declared during the battle, "There is Jackson standing like a stone wall. Let us determine to die here, and we will conquer. Rally behind the Virginians!" It was never ascertained whether this likeness was meant as an insult or a compliment to Jackson, and since Bee died within twenty-four hours after the end of the battle from a shot through the stomach, it was never confirmed whether he spoke these words or what he meant by them. (Whether Bee was, in fact, annoyed with Jackson for not moving forward is not important since both leaders experienced the largest share of the day's fighting. Jackson's brigade fought alone for almost four hours in the eye of the main battle, and they experienced 50 percent of the casualties suffered that day—his actions were later considered particularly heroic.)

McDowell's misgivings about the battle had proved correct, but the federal government felt obliged to remove McDowell from his position at the head of the leading military division due to the failure of the First Battle of Bull Run. McDowell was frank in admitting that he had struggled to coordinate and control his troops on and off the field, enabling the final scramble to DC, during which time he had failed to gather and calm the soldiers in the aftermath of the battle. McDowell's plan had been ambitious and complicated, and it was further exacerbated by his never having led such a large body of troops before. But then again, nobody in the country ever had! McDowell was also later criticized for having engaged too personally in the battle rather than acting as a general and coordinating the troops. Beauregard and Johnston on the Southern side had been commended for leading from behind and funneling fresh troops forward, strategically placing them where their impact would be best. The Southerners' bird's-eye view approach to the First Battle of Manassas had ultimately given them the tactical upper hand.

What remained of the Northern Army of Northeastern Virginia was then combined with the troops from Washington under Brigadier General Joseph K. Mansfield (1803-1862, who died during the war), as well as the Shenandoah men under Major General Nathaniel P. Banks (1816-1894). Major General George B. McClellan ("Young Napoleon") was put in charge of these combined troops, which were known as the main US Army of the Potomac from thereon. McClellan was attributed with training and organizing the Army of the Potomac before being appointed as the commanding general of the US Army in November of that same year. However, McClellan's leadership did not last long, and he was removed from his position in March of the following year, 1862. McClellan did not share the same views on politics or war strategy with President Lincoln; in fact, he even ran against Lincoln as the opposing Democratic nominee in the 1864 presidential elections. After being removed, McClellan would not serve as a military leader in the field again. Despite McClellan's fall from grace, he is attributed with rallying the crucial Army of the Potomac, whose numbers swelled from 50,000 to 168,000 during the four months of his involvement—the largest military force the US had raised until that point. He is also attributed with significantly fortifying the capital with forts, artillery, and cannons to the extent that the city was considered "impregnable."

The battle had been the largest and bloodiest in US history until that point. The First Battle of Bull Run cost the Confederacy 387 fatalities, 1,582 wounded, and 13 missing men. The Union Army had lost 460 men, 1,124 wounded, and a significant 1,312 were missing—assumed captured. (During the entire Civil War, an estimated 620,000 to 850,000 military deaths were recorded, and almost 60 percent of these were Union deaths.)

At the site of Sudley Church, just north of Sudley Springs, the congregation had had the foresight to cancel their morning services as thousands of Union troops and artillery crossed the ford on July 21st, 1861. Later that day, the church would be the scene of a makeshift Union hospital and graveyard for wounded and dead men. Three hundred injured Federal troops were abandoned at the church due to a lack of sufficient transportation. When the Confederates eventually caught up with the retreating enemy near Sudley, they apparently found too many Yankees to capture and hold successfully, so they eventually gave up on taking prisoners. The wounded who were not captured by the Confederates near Sudley Church and who did not die were aided by the church members and their neighbors. Private John Rice, whose life was saved, returned in 1886 to pay for the rebuilding of the church, which was completely destroyed in the Second Battle of Manassas.

After the Battle of First Manassas, the Confederates retained their defensive position within the safety of the Southern states and made no move to attack the capital, although it was feared by many Northerners. The Southern military was in disarray, too, even though the field and the victory had been theirs. The South had won this first significant encounter, but leaders and soldiers of both sides were considerably humiliated, learning what arrogance and inexperience could get them. The Southern celebrations were subdued as the Confederate President Jefferson Davis announced from Richmond,

"We have won a glorious though dear-bought victory. Night closed on the enemy in full flight and closely pursued." Johnston was employed to build the main Southern Army of Northern Virginia, which continued as the South's bastion for the duration of the war.

The collateral damages of the four-year-long war to come, which would include rampant disease, homelessness, economic ruin, the loss of civilian life, destruction of historical buildings and essential farmlands, and, most critically, the loss of able-bodied men (whether they be sons, fathers, etc.), were not considered. After the First Battle of Manassas ended, both Northerners and Southerners withdrew to lick their wounds and rebuild their armies for further onslaughts.

# Conclusion

Ultimately, the Northerners' defeat at Bull Run in the summer of 1861 filled the Southerners with false confidence that they could "lick the Yankees" at every turn. The inexperience and under-preparedness of the Federal forces became starkly apparent. The Southerners, fighting mostly for loyalty and honor, which were connected to deep family ties and old social principles, were, at first, perhaps stronger opponents and more brazen, and they were seemingly more disciplined in this first confrontation. Since it was the North's intention to remove the Southerners' right to own slaves, the Civil War was more personal for the Southerners as their way of life was being threatened.

On both sides of the Mason-Dixon Line, war veterans had predicted the spate of unsteady and cavalier battles that marked the first few years of the Civil War and knew from experience that the war would be neither short nor certain. Civilians alike, who had brought their private carriages and picnics to oversee the battle as a form of entertainment, were shocked and traumatized by the brutality of what unfolded and what this meant going forward. Americans realized they might be living through a real war with gruesome consequences on both sides.

The rapid and glorious victory expected by both assailants at the start of the Civil War never materialized; instead, the First Battle of Manassas was a prelude to the four-year-long bloody outcome of the American Civil War. In an age before rapid media responses or definitive intelligence networks, rumors steeped upon rumors, and ignorance mounted amongst soldiers and civilians alike, creating an atmosphere of confusion and belligerence that laid the foundations for the war to come. On both sides, inaccurate and premature news of victory ran like wildfire through the affected states and was even used as untrue propaganda by the Northern and Southern presses.

This first major land engagement of the Civil War was typical of the chaotic and premature battles during the first year or two of the Civil War, demonstrating that the fighting units were undertrained and uncoordinated. Men were assigned piecemeal, without an awareness of allied units or how to protect one another. Attacks were frontal and unnecessarily brutal with higher than necessary fatalities. Tactical intelligence, most specifically a lack of adequate maps, was slow, inconsistent, and sometimes entirely absent. Finally, battlegrounds were poorly chosen and difficult to navigate. The First Battle of Bull Run initiated military operations in what became known as the Eastern Theater—the battles east of the Appalachian Mountains, including West Virginia, Virginia, the District of Columbia (DC), Maryland, the northern seaports of North Carolina, and Pennsylvania. (The Western Theater included the southern states of Dixieland, between the Mississippi River to the west and the Appalachian Mountains to the east. A further three theaters were named in which key battles of the war occurred.)

The Battle of First Manassas was the first of seven major Civil War battles of the Western Theater, and the state of Virginia would prove to be the site of some of the bloodiest fighting of the American Civil War. Ironically, the old stalwart state of Virginia had at first resisted secession from the Union because of loyalties that linked back to the founding of America in 1776. It was one of the last regions to join the

Confederacy, and divisions in opinion eventually led to the creation of West Virginia in 1863, which split from its home state to join the Union.

The refusal of the South to negotiate the abolition of slavery or some sort of reasonable intercession of its gradual dismantling had prompted the American Civil War, although there were other factors behind the war. The natural loyalties of the Southerners to one another and to their home states—regardless of their opinions about slavery—drew them indiscriminately toward the battle lines. Thus, many American military men who had fought side by side for decades ended their careers as they faced old comrades and colleagues.

Ultimately, the North won, and slavery was abolished, but in the process, the country lost one of its finest presidents, and the South lost its dignity and faced economic and social collapse. The whole of America became responsible for filling the void left by the devastation of the war. If the First Battle of Manassas had taught the two sides anything, it would have been to negotiate and not to fight, but unfortunately, this first real engagement of the war instead stoked the fires of both sides.

Here's another book by Captivating History that you might like

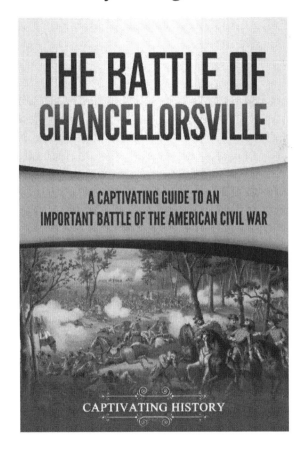

# Free Bonus from Captivating History (Available for a Limited time)

Hi History Lovers!

Now you have a chance to join our exclusive history list so you can get your first history ebook for free as well as discounts and a potential to get more history books for free! Simply visit the link below to join.

Captivatinghistory.com/ebook

Also, make sure to follow us on Facebook, Twitter and Youtube by searching for Captivating History.

# References

American Battlefield Trust:

*Washington, D.C. during the Civil War,*
https://www.battlefields.org/learn/articles/washington-dc-during-civil-war, accessed June 2021.

Battlefields.org:
*An End to Innocence, The First Battle of Manassas,*
https://www.battlefields.org/learn/articles/end-innocence, accessed June 2021,

*The Battle of Bull Run, First Manassas,*
https://www.battlefields.org/learn/articles/bull-run, accessed June 2021,

*Fairfax County and Prince William County, VA, July 21 1861,*
https://www.battlefields.org/learn/civil-war/battles/bull-run, accessed June 2021.

Britannica.com:
*First Battle of Bull Run,* https://www.britannica.com/event/First-Battle-of-Bull-Run-1861, accessed June 2021,

Gould, Kevin, 2015. *Balloon Corps,*
https://www.britannica.com/topic/Balloon-Corps, accessed June 2021.

Furgurson, Ernest B., 2011. *The Civil War, The Battle of Bull Run: The End of Illusions*, accessed via the Smithsonian Magazine, https://www.smithsonianmag.com/history/the-battle-of-bull-run-the-end-of-illusions-17525927/, June 2021.

History.com:
*First Battle of Bull Run*, https://www.history.com/topics/american-civil-war/first-battle-of-bull-run#section_1, accessed June 2021,

:*The First Battle of Bull Run*, https://www.history.com/this-day-in-history/the-first-battle-of-bull-run, accessed June 2021.

National Park Service:
Civil War Series, *The First Battle of Manassas*, Sections 1-7,

https://www.nps.gov/parkhistory/online_books/civil_war_series/17/sec1.htm, accessed

June 2021.

Ruane, Michael E., 2011. *Battle of Bull Run provided a surprising start to the bloody Civil War*, The Washington Post, https://www.washingtonpost.com/local/battle-of-bull-run-provided-a-surprising-start-to-the-bloody-civil-war/2011/06/30/gIQAa7OOGI_story.html, accessed June 2021.

The Ohio State University, *Manassas I (First Bull Run)*,

https://ehistory.osu.edu/battles/manassas-i-first-bull-run, accessed June 2021.

Townsend, Jan, 2011, Ed. Burgess, James. *The Civil War in Prince William County.*, Prince William County Historical Commission, accessed via Prince William County Government, https://www.pwcva.gov/assets/documents/planning/HistComm_Book_The_Civil_War_in_PWC.pdf, June 2021.

Wikipedia: :*Abraham Lincoln,*
https://en.wikipedia.org/wiki/Abraham_Lincoln, accessed June 2021,

*American Civil War*,
https://en.wikipedia.org/wiki/American_Civil_War, accessed June

2021, :*Barnard Elliott Bee Jr.*,
https://en.wikipedia.org/wiki/Barnard_Elliott_Bee_Jr., accessed June 2021,

*Battle of Blackburn's Ford*

*Battle of Fort Sumter*,
https://en.wikipedia.org/wiki/Battle_of_Fort_Sumter, accessed June 2021,

*Charleston Harbor*, https://en.wikipedia.org/wiki/Charleston_Harbor, accessed June 2021,:*Chatham Roberdeau Wheat*,
https://en.wikipedia.org/wiki/Chatham_Roberdeau_Wheat, accessed June 2021,

*Confederate States of America*,
https://en.wikipedia.org/wiki/Confederate_States_of_America, accessed June 2021,

*First Battle of Bull Run*,
https://en.wikipedia.org/wiki/First_Battle_of_Bull_Run, accessed June 2021,

*Francis S Bartow*,
https://en.wikipedia.org/wiki/Francis_S._Bartow#American_Civil_War, accessed June 2021, *George B. McClellan*,
https://en.wikipedia.org/wiki/George_B._McClellan, accessed June 2021,

*Henry House Hill*, https://en.wikipedia.org/wiki/Henry_House_Hill, accessed June 2021,

*List of Weapons of the American Civil War*,
https://en.wikipedia.org/wiki/List_of_weapons_in_the_American_Civil_War, accessed
June 2021,

*Manassas*, https://en.wikipedia.org/wiki/Manassas,_Virginia, accessed June 2021,

---

*Nathan George Evans,*
https://en.wikipedia.org/wiki/Nathan_George_Evans, accessed June 2021,

*P.G.T. Beauregard,*
https://en.wikipedia.org/wiki/P._G._T._Beauregard, accessed June 2021,

*Ordinance of Secession,*
https://en.wikipedia.org/wiki/Ordinance_of_Secession, accessed June 2021,

*Robert Patterson,* https://en.wikipedia.org/wiki/Robert_Patterson, accessed June 2021,

*Union Army Balloon Corps,*
https://en.wikipedia.org/wiki/Union_Army_Balloon_Corps, accessed June 2021,

*Union Army of Potomac,*
https://en.wikipedia.org/wiki/Union_Army_of_the_Potomac, accessed June 2021,

*Winfield Scott,* https://en.wikipedia.org/wiki/Winfield_Scott, accessed June 2021.

# Image References

[1], [3], and [4] Engagement Maps for the First Battle of Bull Run. *Source:* Furgurson, Ernest B., 2011, accessed via the Smithsonian Magazine, *The Civil War, The Battle of Bull Run: The End of Illusions,* https://www.smithsonianmag.com/history/the-battle-of-bull-run-the-end-of-illusions-17525927/, June 2021.

[2] Map of the Battles of Bull Run. *Source:* Bamberger, Solomon, July 21, 1861. West & Johnston, Richmond, Virginia. Property of the U.S. National Archives and Records Administration, accessed via the World Digital Library,

https://www.wdl.org/en/item/2743/, June 2021.

Manufactured by Amazon.ca
Bolton, ON

25230965R00039